GARDEN SQUAD!

IN THE SOIL

DAVE MACK

PowerKiDS press.

New York

Published in 2016 by The Rosen Publishing Group, Inc.
29 East 21st Street, New York, NY 10010

First Edition

Editor: Sarah Machajewski
Book Design: Michael J. Flynn

Photo Credits: Cover (grass and soil) fotoslaz/Shutterstock.com; cover (grubs) Stephen Farhall/Shutterstock.com; cover (earthworms) Barbro Bergfeldt/Shutterstock.com; back cover, pp. 3–4, 6–16, 18, 20, 23–24 (soil) Andrey_Kuzmin/Shutterstock.com; p. 5 Gary John Norman/Digital Vision/Getty Images; p. 7 OlegDoroshin/ Shutterstock.com; p. 9 (bog) gabriel12/Shutterstock.com; p. 9 (desert) Anton_Ivanov/ Shutterstock.com; p. 11 (soil background) Igor Stramyk/Shutterstock.com; p. 11 (soil horizons) Designua/Shutterstock.com; p. 13 (plants) vilax/Shutterstock.com; p. 13 (organic matter) PRILL/Shutterstock.com; p. 13 (bacteria) Juan Gaertner/ Shutterstock.com; p. 13 (fungi) Kichigin/Shutterstock.com; p. 13 (protozoa) Wire_man/Shutterstock.com; p. 13 (mite) Sebastian Kaulitzki/Shutterstock.com; p. 13 (nematode) D. Kucharski K. Kucharska/Shutterstock.com; p. 13 (spider) Olga_Phoenix/Shutterstock.com; p. 13 (earthworm) Vinicius Tupinamba/ Shutterstock.com; p. 13 (beetle) MyImages - Micha/Shutterstock.com; p. 15 wawritto/Shutterstock.com; p. 17 JupiterImages/Photolibrary/Getty Images; p. 19 © iStockphoto.com/martinedoucet; p. 21 (soil testing kit) Sean Maylon/ Photolibrary/Getty Images; p. 21 (soil tester) © iStockphoto.com/samsam62; p. 22 Alexey Losevich/Shutterstock.com.

Library of Congress Cataloging-in-Publication Data

Mack, Dave L., 1955- author.
  In the soil / Dave Mack.
      pages cm. — (Garden squad!)
  Includes bibliographical references and index.
  ISBN 978-1-4994-0975-8 (pbk.)
  ISBN 978-1-4994-0999-4 (6 pack)
  ISBN 978-1-4994-1016-7 (library binding)
  1. Soil ecology—Juvenile literature. 2. Soil formation—Juvenile literature. 3. Soils—Composition—Juvenile literature. I. Title. II. Series: Garden squad!
  QH541.5.S6M33 2016
  577.5'7—dc23
                              2015013120

Manufactured in the United States of America

CPSIA Compliance Information: Batch #WS15PK: For Further Information contact Rosen Publishing, New York, New York at 1-800-237-9932

CONTENTS

A DIRTY JOB 4

MANY KINDS OF MATTER 6

HOW DOES SOIL FORM? 8

LAYERS AND LAYERS 10

IT'S ALIVE! 12

WONDERFUL WORMS 14

CREATING GOOD SOIL 16

NUTRIENT BLAST 18

KEEPING IT HEALTHY 20

A LITTLE EFFORT 22

GLOSSARY 23

INDEX 24

WEBSITES 24

A DIRTY JOB

Gardening is a great outdoor activity. However, like most outdoor activities, you're likely to get pretty dirty while doing it. Your hands, clothes, and skin may be covered with dirt by the time you're done digging and planting your garden.

When you're done gardening, the dirt on your body may seem like nothing more than something to wash off. However, the dirt in your garden is actually a **complex** mixture of living and dead matter. And it's actually not dirt. It's soil! Let's dig into the world of soil to see what it can teach us about gardening.

Understanding soil is a basic part of gardening.

5

MANY KINDS OF MATTER

Soil is very complex. It's made of many different **materials**. Part of it is organic matter. "Organic" means it comes from a living creature. In the case of soil, the organic matter is both dead and alive. The dead stuff comes from **decaying** plants and animals. Tiny **microorganisms**, bugs, and worms are the living part.

Soil also contains nutrients and minerals. Nutrients are matter that's needed in small amounts for living creatures to grow. Minerals are nonliving matter that occurs in nature. Air and water are other important parts of soil. Plants grow best in soil that has a good balance of all these parts.

GARDEN GUIDE

Good soil is light and porous, which means it's full of holes that allow water and air to flow through.

THE PARTS OF SOIL

25%
AIR

45%
MINERALS

25%
WATER

5%
ORGANIC
MATTER

Minerals make up about half of most soils. Air and water make up the other half. Organic matter makes up a tiny part of it. However, every soil is different, and its makeup can change daily.

HOW DOES SOIL FORM?

When you go outside to garden, you may have a backyard full of soil to use. The soil didn't appear out of nowhere. It formed over time from a combination of different elements.

Parent material is the starting point of soil formation. Parent material, such as rocks and organic matter, is the basic stuff needed to make soil. These materials get broken down by weather and other conditions in the **environment**. For example, rain, wind, and strong heat or cold can cause rocks to break apart. The rock pieces get smaller and smaller until they're tiny enough to form soil.

GARDEN GUIDE

Weathering is the process of breaking down rocks. Most soils contain tiny pieces of sand, silt—which is very fine sand—and clay.

WEATHERED ROCKS

PEAT

Weathering can also break down organic matter, such as peat. Peat is a brown, soil-like material that contains partly decayed plant matter.

LAYERS AND LAYERS

Soil is made of **layers** that go 6 feet (1.8 m) below the Earth's surface. The layers are called horizons. You'll only garden in the first two layers. The top layer is the O horizon. This is where most **decomposing** matter is found—it's not quite soil yet. The nutrient-rich A horizon is next. Called topsoil, this is the layer in which your seeds will sprout and your plant roots will grow.

The next layer is the B horizon, or subsoil. It's rich in minerals. The bottom layers are the C horizon, which is typically the parent material, and the R horizon, which is called bedrock.

> When the C and R horizons are exposed by weathering, they provide the parent material for new layers of soil.

O horizon — decomposing matter
A horizon — topsoil
B horizon — subsoil
C horizon — parent material
R horizon — bedrock

The C and R horizons were once the O and A horizons. Existing layers move down as new layers are added and compressed, or pressed tightly together.

IT'S ALIVE!

As weather conditions break down soil's parent material, the tiny pieces of matter build up in layers on the ground. At this point, microorganisms take over. They make soil better for growing plants.

Soil contains thousands of kinds of microorganisms, such as **bacteria** and **fungi**. Though they're too tiny to see, they have a very important job. These decomposers feed on dead plants and animals. Microorganisms called protozoa, worms called nematodes, and bugs are other soil decomposers. As they eat, the microorganisms return nutrients to the soil. Plants need these to grow. Without microorganisms, the soil wouldn't be healthy.

GARDEN GUIDE

"Tilth" is a word that tells if soil is good for planting seeds and supporting plant life. Microorganisms improve tilth.

THE SOIL FOOD WEB

plants

organic matter

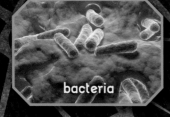
bacteria

fungi

protozoa

mites

nematodes

spiders

earthworms

beetles

Microorganisms are part of a soil **food web**. They feed on the soil and then become food for other microorganisms or bigger animals.

WONDERFUL WORMS

If there's one creature gardeners need, it's earthworms. They care for the soil just by living in it. It's like having a bunch of extra gardeners helping you—for free!

Earthworms are decomposers. They feed on soil and the microorganisms in it, such as bacteria, fungi, and protozoa. As they eat, they leave behind nutrient-rich waste called casts. The casts make the soil better.

Earthworms are also important because they create holes in the soil as they burrow, or dig. This allows air and water to pass through the soil easily. The holes also make room for more plant roots to grow.

Earthworms help "turn over" the soil. That means they mix it. It's similar to a gardener breaking up soil with a shovel.

GARDEN GUIDE

Earthworms aren't in all kinds of healthy soil, but earthworms are a sign that soil is healthy.

CREATING GOOD SOIL

Good soil is the most important part of growing a successful garden. You can't just dig a hole in the ground and expect your plants to grow. You need to work with your yard's soil to make it good for growing.

The first step is to choose a spot for your garden. Next, get digging. Dig anywhere from 6 to 12 inches (15 to 30 cm) deep—this puts you in the O and A horizons. Break up large chunks of soil with your shovel. Turn it over by bringing the bottom layers to the top. This will loosen the soil and allow air to enter.

GARDEN GUIDE

Water your soil after you've dug it up. Allow it to dry before planting.

Good soil is light, loose, and moist. Plants won't grow well in hard, compact, or dry soil.

NUTRIENT BLAST

The soil in your backyard might be good to begin with. It will be even better if you add nutrient-rich materials to it. They're called soil **amendments**. One of the best examples is compost.

Compost is a mixture of decayed organic material, such as food scraps and plant trimmings. Microorganisms turn it into dark, earthy-smelling matter that's full of nutrients. Other soil amendments include leaves, tree bark, peat moss, and topsoil. Make sure to mix them throughout your entire garden bed—mixing them deep into the soil means your plants' roots will have plenty of nutrients, water, and air.

Some gardeners take the extra step and make their own compost. It's easy, free, and fun!

COMPOST
BIN

19

KEEPING IT HEALTHY

Once your soil is ready to go, it's time to start planting. Your seeds will sprout and grow into adult plants in just a short time. However, a gardener's work doesn't end there. Gardens need care—and not just for the plants. Soil needs care, too.

Plants take all the nutrients and water out of the soil as they grow. If your soil seems too dry, give it a good watering. Make sure it's loose and light enough for air to flow through. Add new organic material such as compost to make sure worms and microorganisms have enough to eat.

GARDEN GUIDE

At the end of a gardening season, your soil will probably have few nutrients left. It's important to turn it over and add nutrients before your next round of planting.

pH Test ①

pH 8.0

pH 7.0

pH 6.0

pH 5.0

FRUIT AND FLOWERS

These tools are used to test soil quality, or how good it is. Gardeners use them so they don't waste time or money planting in bad soil.

A LITTLE EFFORT

Soil is the first building block of a great garden. When your garden is full of loose, damp, and nutrient-rich soil, your plants have the best chance of growing healthy and strong. Unlike people, plants can't move around to find food. We can help them by making their soil full of the air, water, and nutrients they need to survive.

Preparing gardening soil takes a little bit of effort, but it's worth it. The best way to get started is to dig right in. You may be surprised at the secret life your garden's soil holds.

GLOSSARY

amendment: Organic matter added to soil to improve it.

bacteria: Tiny creatures that can be seen only with a microscope.

compact: Pressed together.

complex: Made of many parts.

decay: To rot.

decompose: To rot. Also, to break something down, such as when bacteria or fungi feed on decaying matter.

environment: The natural world in which a plant or animal lives.

food web: A drawing or plan that shows the flow of energy among living things in an environment.

fungi: Living things that are somewhat like a plant, but don't make their own food, have leaves, or have a green color. Fungi include molds and mushrooms. The singular form is "fungus."

layer: One thickness laying over or under another.

material: The matter from which something is made.

microorganism: A tiny creature that can only be seen with a microscope.

INDEX

A
air, 6, 7, 14, 16, 18, 20, 22
amendments, 18

B
bacteria, 12, 13, 14
bedrock, 10, 11

C
casts, 14
compost, 18, 19, 20

D
decomposers, 12, 14
decomposing matter, 10, 11

E
earthworms, 6, 13, 14, 15, 20

F
fungi, 12, 13, 14

H
horizons, 10, 11, 16

M
microorganisms, 6, 12, 13, 14, 18, 20
minerals, 6, 7, 10

N
nematodes, 12, 13
nutrients, 6, 10, 12, 14, 18, 20, 22

O
organic matter, 6, 7, 8, 9, 13, 18, 20

P
parent material, 8, 10, 11, 12
protozoa, 12, 13, 14

R
rocks, 8, 9

S
soil food web, 13
subsoil, 10, 11

T
topsoil, 10, 11, 18

W
water, 6, 7, 14, 16, 18, 20, 22
weathering, 8, 9, 10, 12

WEBSITES

Due to the changing nature of Internet links, PowerKids Press has developed an online list of websites related to the subject of this book. This site is updated regularly. Please use this link to access the list: www.powerkidslinks.com/grdn/soil